The Runaway Sheep

Written by DAN OLSON
Illustrated by CRAIG MACINTOSH

"What do you think? If a man owns a hundred sheep, and one of them wanders away, will he not leave the ninety-nine on the hills and go to look for the one that wandered off?"

MATTHEW 18:12

There was once a little sheep who decided to run away.

She said to the good shepherd, "I am running away."

"If you run away," said the shepherd,

"I will come and find you. For you are my little sheep."

"If you come after me," said the little sheep, "I will become a flower and hide myself in the shade of the trees in a garden."

"If you become a flower and hide
in a garden," said the shepherd,
"I will be a gardener,
and walk in the cool of the day.
And I will find you."

"If you become a gardener and find me,"
said the little sheep,
"I'll become an olive branch on a tree,
high on the hills above you."

"If you become an
olive branch on a hill,"
said the shepherd,
"I'll become a dove
and fly up to you
and bring you
back to me."

“If you become a
dove and find me,”
said the little sheep,
“I'll become a diver and
dive down to the depths
of the darkest sea.”

“If you become a diver in the depths of the sea,”
said the shepherd,
“I'll become a whale and swallow you
and I will carry you to dry land.”

NINEVEH
EGYPT
DAMASCUS
JERUSALEM
ATHENS

"If you become a whale,"

said the sheep,

"I will become a stubborn ox

and plow in a field far away from you."

"If you become an ox,"
said the shepherd,
"I will become a baby in a manger,
and we will be together
in the warmth of the hay."

“If you become a baby in a manger,”
said the sheep,
“I will become a grown-up
and I will deny you.”

"If you grow up and deny me,"
said the shepherd,
"I will become a rooster
and will crow three times,
and you will remember me."

"If you become a rooster and
crow three times," said the sheep,
"I will become a boat
and sail away from you."

"If you become a boat and sail from me,"
said the shepherd,
"I will become a storm and blow and cause
the waves to bring you back to me."

MALTA

"If you become a storm
and blow me to shore,"
said the sheep,
"I will hide from you
in a deep dark tomb."

"Even if you hide from me in the depths of the grave," said the shepherd, "I will wake you up and set you free."

"Well... ," said the sheep,

"then I think that I will stay right here

and be your little sheep."

"Rest in me," said the shepherd.

And so she did.

"But ask the animals, and they will teach you,
or the birds in the sky, and they will tell you;
or speak to the earth, and it will teach you,
or let the fish in the sea inform you.
Which of all these does not know
that the hand of the LORD has done this?"

JOB 12:7-9

For Drew, and all 'dialectical opposites' everywhere - DAN OLSON

Listen to a sample from "The Shepherd's Lullaby"
by Jake Armerding (with Dan Olson)
a bedtime song inspired by The Runaway Sheep

ISBN: 978-1-915705-62-4

Published by 10Publishing, a division of 10ofThose Limited, Tomlinson Road, Leyland, Lancs, PR25 2DY, England
info@10ofthose.com   www.10ofthose.com

Written by Dan Olson   Illustrated by Craig MacIntosh   Designed by Diane Warnes

1 3 5 7 9 10 8 6 4 2